Great National Soccer Teams / Grandes selecciones del fútbol mundial

ITALY / ITALIA

José María Obregón

English translation: Megan Benson

Editorial Buenas Letras™
New York

Published in 2010 by The Rosen Publishing Group, Inc.
29 East 21st Street, New York, NY 10010

First Edition

Editor: Nicole Pristash
Book Design: Julio Gil
Photo Researcher: Jessica Gerweck

Photo Credits: Cover, pp. 5, 21 (middle, right) AFP/Getty Images; back cover Bob Thomas/Getty Images; p. 7 Alex Livesey/Getty Images; pp. 9, 13, 15 Popperfoto/Getty Images; pp. 11, 17, 19, 21 (left) Getty Images; p. 21 (flag) Shutterstock.com.

Library of Congress Cataloging-in-Publication Data

Obregón, José María, 1963–
    Italy = Italia / José María Obregón. — 1st ed.
        p. cm. — (Great national soccer teams = Grandes selecciones nacionales de fútbol)
    Includes index.
    ISBN 978-1-4042-8086-1 (library binding) — ISBN 978-1-4358-2491-1 (pbk.) — ISBN 978-1-4358-2492-8 (6-pack)
    1. Soccer—Italy—Juvenile literature. 2. Soccer teams—Italy—Juvenile literature. I. Title. II. Title: Italia.
    GV944.I8O37 2010
    796.334'640945—dc22
                                                            2008052690

Manufactured in the United States of America

CONTENTS

CONTENIDO

Italy's national soccer team is one of the best soccer teams in the world. Italy has won the **World Cup** four times. Italian players Giuseppe Meazza, Luigi Riva, Roberto Baggio, and Paolo Maldini are among the best players ever to play the game.

La selección de fútbol de Italia es uno de los mejores equipos de fútbol del mundo. Italia ha ganado la **Copa del Mundo** en cuatro ocasiones. Jugadores italianos como Giuseppe Meazza, Luigi Riva, Roberto Baggio y Paolo Maldini se encuentran entre los mejores jugadores en la historia del fútbol.

The Italian team is shown here enjoying their World Cup win in 2006.

La selección de Italia celebra tras ganar la final de la Copa del Mundo 2006.

Italy's players have great strength and skill. They are very good at **defending** their goal. It is hard to score a goal against them! The team is known as the Azzurri because the players wear blue jerseys, or team shirts. *Azzurro* means "blue" in Italian.

La selección italiana juega de color azul por lo que se la conoce como los Azzurri. *Azzurro* es azul en italiano. El estilo de juego italiano se basa en la fuerza y en la habilidad de sus jugadores. Los Azzurri son muy buenos **defendiendo** su meta. ¡Es muy difícil meterles un gol!

Italian player Gennaro Gattuso (number 8, in blue) fights for the ball with Florent Malouda, of France.

Gennaro Gattuso (número 8, en azul) pelea por el balón con el jugador francés, Florent Malouda.

7

Italy's first great player was Giuseppe Meazza. Meazza helped the Azzurri win their first World Cup in 1934. Four years later, at the World Cup France, Meazza was team captain. Italy won, becoming the first country to win two World Cups back to back.

Giuseppe Meazza fue el primer gran jugador italiano. Meazza ayudó a los Azzurri a ganar su primera Copa del Mundo en 1934. Cuatro años más tarde, en Francia 1938, con Meazza como capitán, Italia se convirtió en el primer país en ganar dos copas del mundo consecutivas.

The Italian team is seen here carrying coach Vittorio Pozzo after their World Cup win in 1934.

El equipo italiano levanta al entrenador Vittorio Pozzo tras su victoria en la Copa del Mundo, en 1934.

9

The year 1949 was a sad year for soccer. An airplane carrying Italian soccer players crashed during landing. Eighteen players, many of them members of the national team, died. That year, and for the following 20 years, Italy did not win any big **tournaments**.

1949 fue un año muy triste para el fútbol. El avión en el que viajaban muchos jugadores italianos se estrelló al aterrizar. En el accidente murieron 18 jugadores, muchos de los cuales formaban parte de la selección nacional. Italia no ganaría otro **torneo** importante en veinte años.

Shown here is the scene of the plane crash on Superga, a hill outside Turin, Italy.

La escena del accidente en la montaña Superga, en las afueras de la ciudad italiana de Turín.

In 1968, the UEFA European Football Championship was held in Italy. The Azzurri reached the final game, playing against the Yugoslavian national team. The game ended tied, 1–1, and the final score had to be decided in a second match. Italy won, 2–0.

En 1968, Italia organizó la Copa de Europa. Los Azzurri llegaron a la final en contra de la selección de Yugoslavia. El partido quedó empatado a un gol, y la final tuvo que ser decidida en otro juego. Italia ganó el segundo partido 2 a 0.

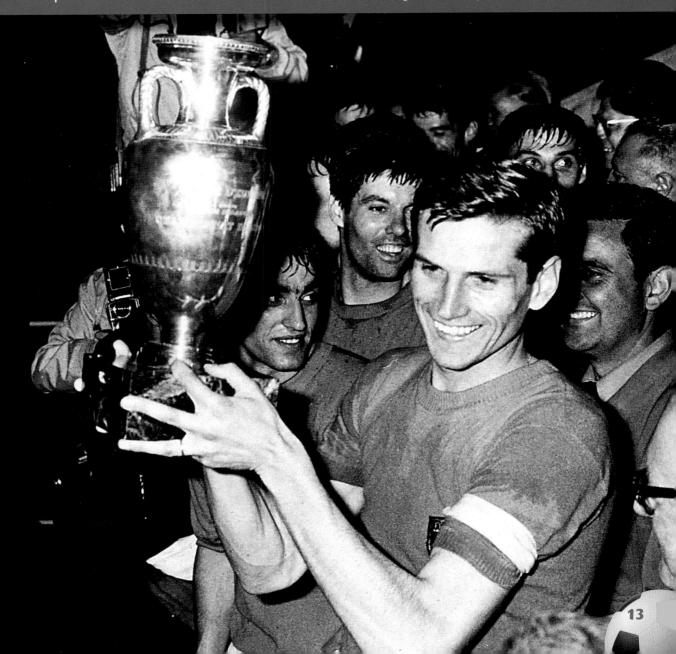

Italian captain Giacinto Facchetti lifts the trophy after winning the European Football Championship in 1968.

El capitán italiano Giacinto Facchetti levanta el trofeo tras ganar la Copa de Europa.

During the World Cup Mexico 1970, Italy played against Germany in an exciting semifinal match known as the Game of the Century. The game went into overtime, or extra time added to the end of the game. Italy won, 4–3. However, Italy lost the final game to Brazil.

Durante la Copa del Mundo de México 1970, Italia jugó contra Alemania el llamado juego del siglo. Los equipos jugaban la semifinal de la copa, y el ganador jugaría la final contra Brasil. El partido se decidió en tiempos extras e Italia ganó por 4 a 3. Sin embargo, Italia perdió la final con Brasil.

Here you can see Italian and German players during the Game of the Century, in Azteca Stadium.

La acción durante el juego del siglo, realizado en el Estadio Azteca en la Ciudad de México.

15

Italy pressed on and won its third World Cup in Spain in 1982. **Striker** Paolo Rossi scored six goals in the tournament. In 1990, the World Cup returned to Italy. The Azzurri were the favored team to win, but they had to settle for third place.

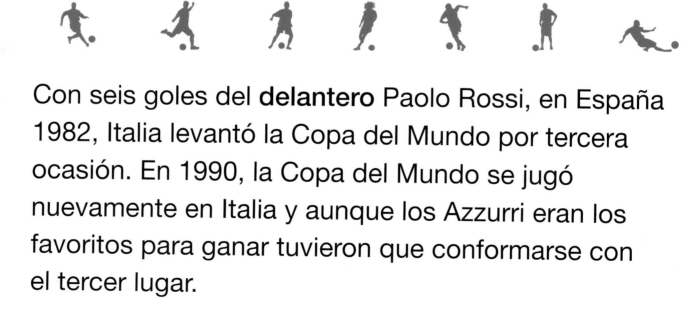

Con seis goles del **delantero** Paolo Rossi, en España 1982, Italia levantó la Copa del Mundo por tercera ocasión. En 1990, la Copa del Mundo se jugó nuevamente en Italia y aunque los Azzurri eran los favoritos para ganar tuvieron que conformarse con el tercer lugar.

Paolo Rossi (center) led the Italian team to a World Cup win in 1982.

Paolo Rossi (centro) llevó al equipo italiano a ganar la Copa del Mundo de 1982.

17

Of all of Italy's players, no one shows the greatness of Italian soccer as much as Paolo Maldini does. Maldini has played 126 games with the national team, and he has scored seven goals. Maldini has also played for Milan, an Italian team, for 25 years. Maldini is a star!

Ningún otro jugador representa la grandeza del fútbol italiano como Paolo Maldini. Maldini ha jugado durante 25 años con el equipo de Milán. Con la selección nacional, ha jugado 126 partidos y anotado 7 goles. ¡A los 40 años, Maldini sigue siendo una estrella Azzurri!

Paolo Maldini, shown here, is one of the best defenders in soccer history.

Paolo Maldini ha sido uno de los mejores defensas en la historia del fútbol.

19

In 2006, the Azzurri played against France in the final game of the World Cup in Germany. The game ended tied, 1–1, but Italy won after a **penalty shoot-out**. This was Italy's fourth World Cup win, making the team one of the greatest teams in soccer.

En 2006, los Azzurri enfrentaron a Francia en la final de la Copa del Mundo, en Alemania. El partido terminó empatado a un gol, pero Italia ganó en **serie de penales**. Así, Italia ganó su cuarta Copa del Mundo convirtiéndose en uno de los mejores equipos de la historia.

ITALY

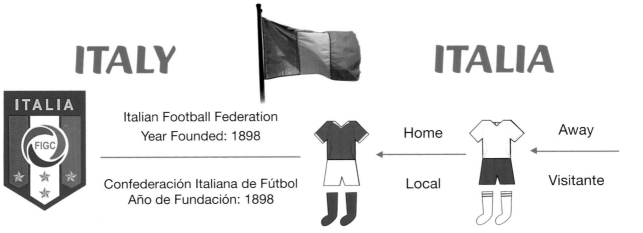

ITALIA

Italian Football Federation
Year Founded: 1898

Confederación Italiana de Fútbol
Año de Fundación: 1898

Home
Local

Away
Visitante

Player Highlights / Jugadores destacados

Most Caps* / Más convocatorias

Paolo Maldini (1988–2002)
126 caps / 126 convocatorias

Top Scorer / Mejor anotador

Luigi Riva (1965–1974)
35 goals / 35 goles

Top Goalie / Mejor portero

Gianluigi Buffon (1997–   )
FIFA World Cup: Champion 2006 /
Copa del Mundo FIFA: Campeón 2006

* Appearances with the national soccer team

Team Highlights / Palmarés del equipo

FIFA World Cup™/ Copa Mundial FIFA
  Appearances / Participaciones: 16
  Winner / Ganador: 1934, 1938, 1982, 2006
  Runner-Up / Segundo: 1970, 1994
  Third / Tercero: 1990

UEFA European Football Championship /
Eurocopa UEFA
  Winner / Ganador: 1968
  Runner-Up / Segundo: 2000

1936 Olympics / Olimpíadas de 1936
  Gold Medal / Medalla de Oro

GLOSSARY / GLOSARIO

defending (dih-FEND-ing) Trying to keep the other team from scoring a goal.

penalty shoot-out (PEH-nul-tee SHOOT-owt) Players from each team try to score a goal in turn until one player fails to score. That player's team loses the game.

striker (STRY-ker) A player who scores goals.

tournaments (TOR-nuh-ments) A group of games to decide the best team.

World Cup (WUR-uld KUP) A group of games that takes place every four years with teams from around the world.

Copa del Mundo (la) Competencia de fútbol, cada 4 años, en la que juegan los mejores equipos del mundo.

defender Evitar que el otro equipo anote goles.

delantero (el) Un jugador que anota goles.

serie de penales (la) Cuando un partido se decide con los jugadores tirando, en turnos, a la portería. El jugador que falla pierde el partido.

torneo (el) Un grupo de partidos que deciden cuál es el mejor equipo.

RESOURCES / RECURSOS

Books in English / Libros en inglés

Crawford, Andy. *Soccer*. New York: DK Publishing, 2005.

Minden, Cecilia. *Soccer*. Ann Arbor, MI: Cherry Lake Publishing, 2009.

Books in Spanish / Libros en español

Contró, Arturo. *Gianluigi Buffon*. New York: PowerKids Press/Editorial Buenas Letras, 2008.

Dann, Sarah. *Fútbol en acción (Soccer in Action)*. New York: Crabtree Publishing, 2005.

Web Sites

Due to the changing nature of Internet links, PowerKids Press has developed an online list of Web sites related to the subject of this book. This site is updated regularly. Please use this link to access the list:
www.powerkidslinks.com/soct/italy/

23

INDEX

ÍNDICE